PRE TEEN PRESSURES

DEATH

by Barbara Sprung

RSVP

RAINTREE
STECK-VAUGHN
PUBLISHERS
The Steck-Vaughn Company

Austin, Texas

Consultants

Rita Joy Coslet, Social Worker, Family Service Association of Bucks County, PA

William B. Presnell, Clinical Member, American Association for Marriage and Family Therapy

Developed for Steck-Vaughn Company by
Visual Education Corporation, Princeton, New Jersey

Project Director: Jewel Moulthrop
Editor: Paula McGuire
Editorial Assistant: Jacqueline Morais
Photo Research: Sara Matthews
Electronic Preparation: Cynthia C. Feldner, Manager; Fiona Torphy
Production Supervisor: Ellen Foos
Electronic Production: Lisa Evans-Skopas, Manager; Elise Dodeles, Deirdre Sheean, Isabelle Verret
Interior Design: Maxson Crandall

Raintree Steck-Vaughn Publishers staff

Editor: Kathy DeVico
Project Manager: Joyce Spicer

Photo Credits: Cover: © Jean Higgins/Unicorn Stock Photos; 6: © Michael Newman/ PhotoEdit; 10: © David Young-Wolff/PhotoEdit; 13: © Tony Freeman/PhotoEdit; 15: © Tony Freeman/PhotoEdit; 16: © Paul Conklin/PhotoEdit; 20: © Jean Higgins/ Unicorn Stock Photos; 23: © Gary L. Johnson/Unicorn Stock Photos; 24: © David Young-Wolff/PhotoEdit; 31: © Jeff Greenberg/Unicorn Stock Photos; 33: © Tony Freeman/ PhotoEdit; 35: © David Young-Wolff/PhotoEdit; 40: © Michael Newman/PhotoEdit; 41: © Tony Freeman/PhotoEdit; 44: © Skjold Photographs

Library of Congress Cataloging-in-Publication Data

Sprung, Barbara.
    Death/by Barbara Sprung.
       p.   cm. — (Preteen pressures)
    Includes bibliographical references and index.
    Summary: Discusses what it feels like to experience the death of a loved one, outlines the stages of grief and mourning, and describes ways to honor or remember someone who has died.
    ISBN 0-8172-5029-8
    1. Death—Psychological aspects—Juvenile literature. 2. Grief in children— Juvenile literature. 3. Bereavement in children—Juvenile literature. [1. Death. 2. Grief.]   I. Title. II. Series.
BF789.D4S67
155.9'37—dc21
                                                 97-37299
                                                    CIP
                                                     AC

Printed and bound in the United States
1 2 3 4 5 6 7 8 9 0 LB 01 00 99 98 97

CONTENTS

Introduction **4**

The End of a Long Life **7**

The Death of a Parent **13**

Sudden Death **21**

Suicide **25**

Feeling Grief **31**

Coping with Death **37**

Glossary **45**

Where to Go for Help **46**

For More Information **47**

Index **48**

INTRODUCTION

Death is a difficult subject to talk about, for grown-ups as well as for preteens. We learn at an early age that people and all other living things die, and that death is the natural end to life. Like the leaves on the trees that are green in spring and change color and die when autumn comes, all other forms of life die as well.

Sometimes when we are young, and an elderly relative dies, our parents use the occasion to explain the meaning of death. Still, it is difficult for most of us to deal with the idea that someone we knew well is gone forever. The person will live in our memory, but she or he can no longer be a part of our everyday life. This realization causes us to feel a deep sense of loss, especially if the person who died was someone we dearly loved. We will find that the sense of loss becomes less over time, but it may never go away completely.

This book was written to help you understand and cope with the loss of someone you loved. Each of the first four chapters deals with a different kind of death: the death of an older family member; the death of a parent; an unexpected death; and a death by suicide (when a person ends his or her own life). The fifth chapter is about the feelings and emotions that you may experience when someone dies—grief, sadness, anger, confusion, disbelief, and fear. The last chapter is about different ways in which people grieve and learn to cope with the death of someone they love. Each chapter begins with a story about a preteen who has experienced the death of someone close. At the back of the book, there are resources—books to read and places to call—that can help you and your family during a time of loss. We hope you will find these resources helpful. Remember that your library is always a good source for additional information. Librarians can help you find the names of support groups, counselors, and religious groups or other organizations in your area that can help you cope with loss. This will not be an easy topic to read about, but we hope that you will find the book informative and useful.

Coping with the death of a loved one for the first time is likely to be very difficult.

THE END OF A LONG LIFE

Jen is 11 years old. Her grandmother, who was 83, died three days ago. The funeral took place this morning. It was the first time Jen had ever been to a funeral. When her grandfather died four years ago, Jen was only seven. Her parents had thought that she was too young to understand about death and that funerals were too sad for children. So Jen stayed at a friend's house for the whole day.

This time, when Grandma died, Jen said that she wanted to go to the funeral, and her parents said it was OK. Jen and her grandmother had been very close. Grandma had heart disease, and she had to take a lot of medicine to keep her heart beating regularly. But she still led a pretty busy life. Whenever she felt well enough, she helped out in the library, which was down the street from her house. Grandma would visit Jen and her family every week, usually on Sunday. Jen called her on the telephone almost every day. They chatted about school, about Grandma's volunteer work at the library, about anything and everything. Jen loved her grandmother and felt that she was a special friend, the kind you could tell all your secrets to.

After the funeral, many people came back to Jen's house. Some were family friends, but some of the people were strangers to Jen. Everyone was eating and drinking and talking. Some people were even laughing, which made Jen feel angry.

All Jen wanted to do was curl up next to her mother, but her mother was surrounded by people, and Jen couldn't get near her. She needed comforting, and she knew her mother needed comforting. But that wouldn't happen until all the people went home. Jen was feeling very sad.

A NATURAL DEATH

When a person dies from an illness at the end of a long life, we think of it as a natural death. From the time we are young, we hear people say things like, "Well, Harry lived to a ripe old age. His family was lucky to have him so long." Or, "Mrs. Martin's death was to be expected. She was old and had been sick for a long time."

We know that all living things die. In nature we see plants and animals die. In our families and perhaps in our places of worship, we learn that death is part of the natural order of the universe. But no matter how much we may accept the fact of death in our minds, when a special friend or relative dies, we have a hard time dealing with our feelings. As natural as the death of an older person may seem, it is still an emotionally painful experience to lose someone you love.

Think about this: Your parents are part of your life from the day you are born. They take care of your needs and keep you safe and healthy when you are young. They help you grow up and become independent. They are part of your adult life. When you have children of your own, your parents love them in a very special way—as grandparents.

When your parents grow old, you may have to help them, as they helped you when you were young. It's a long cycle of life that you go through together. So even when you become an independent adult, there will be a tremendous sense of loss when your parents die. It is very hard when death breaks the cycle of your life together.

A young person, too, can feel a similar sense of loss when a grandparent or other close older relative dies. It's hard to think of the future without that person who has been a part of one's life for so long. Maybe the older person and the younger person had a special relationship, like Jen and her grandmother. Older people are family connectors—they are a part of the past and the present. They were there when your parents' generation was young, and they are there for people your age now.

ABOUT TERMINAL ILLNESS

Sometimes an older person, who hasn't shown any signs of illness, dies suddenly. Although family and friends are saddened and shocked when that happens, they may also be relieved that the person didn't have to go through a long, painful illness. But sudden death isn't that common among older persons.

A grandparent can hold a special place in a young person's heart.

A more common occurrence is that an older person develops an illness that eventually leads to his or her death. This is called a terminal illness because the end result is always death. The word *terminal* means "end."

When older people develop terminal illnesses, such as cancer or heart disease, medications and treatment may prolong life for a time, but eventually these diseases cause death. Sometimes people may choose not to take all the expensive, and often unpleasant, treatments available. They may prefer to see death as a natural and welcome end to their suffering. In recent years many people have prepared a document called a living will. A living will provides instructions for family members and doctors in the event that the person becomes too ill to speak for himself or herself. Usually the living will states that the person does not wish to be kept alive on life-support machines, but prefers to let the illness run its natural course.

PREPARING FOR A DEATH

When we know that a relative is very old, or when we learn that she or he has a terminal disease, we begin to prepare ourselves for that person's death. Sometimes this is a long process. For example, perhaps you notice that your grandparent or a favorite aunt or uncle is behaving differently. That person may joke with you less or play games with you less than he or she used to.

Perhaps one of the younger adults in the family (maybe your mom or dad) often drives the person to the doctor's office or to the hospital for brief stays. You may overhear your parents and other adults talking about the illness. You may wish that someone would tell you what is going on. Or, if your family shares information openly, you may know exactly what is happening. Maybe after several visits to the person in the hospital, you begin to think that his or her next hospital stay might be the last one.

You may not realize it, but you are going through a process of separation. Other members of your family are also preparing themselves for the death of a beloved relative. If at all possible, ask your parents about what is happening. Try to talk about it together. It really helps to share your feelings with one another.

Many older people also prepare themselves for the permanent separation from the family that their death will cause. People have many ways to say good-bye. One way is to give a favorite possession to a relative to be remembered by—a watch, a necklace, a stamp collection, fishing gear, books, or a musical instrument. Another way is to arrange a special farewell visit to talk about past times and future hopes for the person left behind. A third way might be to write good-bye letters to close relatives or friends.

Many older people also prepare for death by writing a will. This will is very different from the living will that was already explained. A will provides a legal way to give away the property that a person owned while he or she was alive. And most people have strong feelings about how they want to divide their property among their relatives and friends. Property may include money, a house or land, furniture, jewelry, art—anything that the person owned at the time of his or her death. A person prepares a will with a lawyer, who will keep the will in his or her office. When the person dies, the lawyer will inform the family members and friends who have been left property.

There are many different ways to prepare for the death of an older person. You prepare, and they prepare, for the separation. Still the finality of death creates feelings of sadness and loneliness, and you grieve for the person who has died.

THE DEATH OF A PARENT

It's Saturday morning. Mason and Sandy and their father, Tim, are sitting in the waiting room of the hospital. The boys are trying to play a card game, and their father is trying to read the newspaper. But they aren't paying much attention to what they are doing. Everyone looks tired and stressed out. Mason's eyes are red because he has been crying.

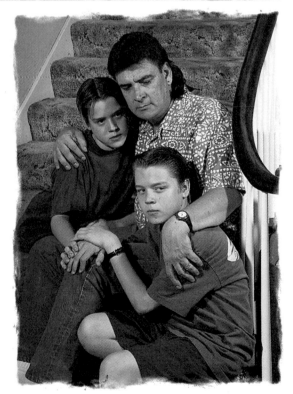

The loss of a parent breaks one of the most important bonds in a young person's life.

Mason and Sandy are used to spending time in this waiting room because their mother, Mary, has been hospitalized five times in the past year. This time she has been in for two weeks, and the family knows that she is not coming home. She is going to die.

About one year ago, Mary wasn't feeling well. She was tired all the time, and she was losing weight. After a while she agreed to go to the family doctor for a check-up. The doctor sent Mary right to the hospital for tests.

When the test results came back, the news was bad. The doctor told Mary and Tim that she had cancer, and that it had advanced to a very serious stage. Mary had about one year to live. Mary and Tim did not hide the facts from Mason and Sandy. They decided that the boys should know, and that the family had to work together through the difficult time they were facing.

Sometimes Mary seemed OK. At other times she was very sick, and she rested most of the day. Knowing that their mom was in pain made the brothers feel very sad. They also felt angry that the doctors had no cure for her type of cancer.

Mason and Sandy tried to help around the house as much as they could. With their father at work all day and their mom in bed, family life seemed pretty disorganized. The boys often felt that it was unfair that they had so many chores. Sometimes at night they would talk about how frightened they felt. They talked about how much they missed the happier times before their mom was so sick.

Now the boys and their father will stay in the hospital with Mary until she dies. The doctor said that it would happen within a few hours. She already has kissed them and she has slipped into a coma, which means that she is unconscious. Tim has tried to reassure his sons that they will always be a family and will help one another through the difficult times ahead.

PREPARING FOR THE DEATH OF A PARENT

Preparing for the loss of a parent sounds like an almost impossible thing for a child to do. Parents are supposed to take care of you until you are a grown-up and able to be on your own. When a parent dies while children are still at home, it seems unnatural. It breaks the order of life that we expect.

If a parent is ill for many months, like Mary, there is time to start preparing for death. During the year that Mary

When a close relative is dying, you may have to take on more responsibilities.

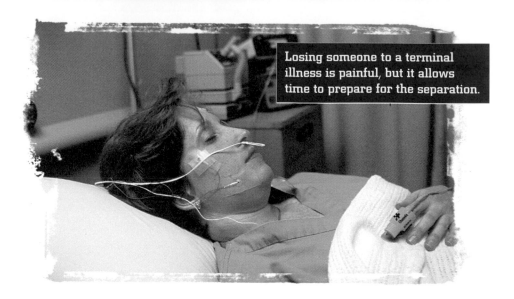

Losing someone to a terminal illness is painful, but it allows time to prepare for the separation.

was sick, Mason and Sandy and their parents had time to talk about their feelings. The boys also adjusted to some of the daily changes that losing one parent would bring. Since their mom was too ill to function some of the time, the brothers learned to take care of themselves while their dad was at work. In this way they were able to prepare themselves a little—both emotionally and practically—for the final separation.

If a parent dies suddenly from a heart attack or in an accident, there is no time to prepare. The shock for the children and the remaining parent is severe, and the adjustment to life afterward can be long and painful. In some ways it may be even more difficult than losing a parent to terminal illness, in which case there has been time to grieve in advance.

DEATH: AN END TO SUFFERING

Did you ever think that death might bring relief? Sometimes when a person has a terminal illness that causes pain, she or he may begin to look at death as an end to suffering. A very sick person may also be aware that his or her illness is causing great suffering for other family members and may desire relief for them.

Mary certainly knew that her children and husband were hurting as they watched her illness progress. That probably added emotional pain to her physical pain. Everyone in the family suffered for a whole year. Finally Mary's death brought an end to her pain. Along with all the sadness her family felt about her death, there probably was also a sense of relief that her suffering was over.

FEELINGS ABOUT LOSING A PARENT

When a parent dies while children are still young, it feels unnatural. The death of a parent gives rise to many feelings, and none of them is pleasant or comfortable. These are some feelings you might have if your parent died:

▶ **Anger.** It is certainly understandable if you feel angry. Your life has changed. One of the most important people in your life—someone you loved and who loved you in return—can never be there for you again. Other kids are not grieving, and you are. Their lives haven't suddenly changed, and yours has.

▶ **Abandonment.** In your mind you know that your parent who died couldn't keep it from happening. But in your heart you may feel abandoned by that parent. You need that parent, and he or she is not there for you. You can't ignore that feeling, and you may feel angry with yourself for feeling this way.

► **Worry.** You may feel worried about what will happen to you after your parent's death. Maybe you are concerned that something bad will happen to your remaining parent. You may be worried that your family will not be able to stay together. You may worry that you will have to move away from your friends. You may even worry that someday you will become sick, too, just like your parent.

► **Disbelief.** When you have to go through such a very difficult experience as the death of a parent, your emotions often go into a kind of shock. You just can't believe that this is happening to you. It seems too unpleasant and unreal. This feeling is also called denial. You "deny" the reality because it hurts too much.

► **Helplessness.** Death is something that you cannot control, and it makes you feel helpless. No matter how much you may want to, you can't save your parent from illness or death. A feeling of helplessness may also come from knowing that you are still too young to take complete care of yourself. You still depend on your parents to give you care and guidance as you grow. This care is something you probably didn't think much about, until your parent died.

► **Embarrassment.** Sometimes when you have an unusual experience, one that sets you apart from all your friends, you feel embarrassed. The death of a parent can be that kind of experience. It is something that most kids don't have to go through. Young people want to be like everyone else, not different. Your friends feel sad for you, but they may not know how to express their sorrow. You want them to be there for you, but you also want things to be as they always were. You may not go to school for a while or play sports, which again sets you apart from your friends and may embarrass you.

All of these feelings are natural for a young person who has lost a parent. They are pretty much the same feelings that adults have when they lose a loved one. Adults, too, can experience anger, abandonment, denial, helplessness, and embarrassment when someone close to them dies.

WHAT HELPS?

As a young person whose parent has died, you have gone through one of life's most difficult experiences. There is no way to deny that. Some people might say things like the following: "You're young, you'll get over it." "Try not to be so sad, you have your whole life in front of you." "Be brave for your dad (or mom) and little sister (or brother)." Although people try to be comforting and kind, these remarks are usually not helpful.

What may help you in your time of grief is to find someone you can talk to about all the emotions you are feeling. Find a person who will listen and understand without telling you how you should feel or act. That person may be your remaining parent, a sister or brother, another relative, a friend, a pastor, priest, or rabbi, a counselor, or a therapist.

It also helps if you and your family are close and supportive of one another at this time. You have shared the

In times of grief, people do not always know the right things to say to comfort someone.

death of someone you loved, and now you are sharing the grief. You all need to know that you are still a family. You also need to plan together how you will function as a family from this time on. So communicating with each other is very important. It may not be easy. Some people have a hard time talking about their feelings, especially when they are sad. But if you and your family can talk to one another, it will help all of you to cope.

Time also helps. Everyone needs time to recover from the death of a loved one. No one can predict how much time it will take to heal the sorrow. Some people seem able to go on with their daily activities fairly quickly. Others take many months, or even years, to return to a former routine. Accepting the emotions you are feeling is the first step toward eventual relief, no matter how long it takes.

Carrie, Jody, Cheryl, Josh, and Ben are sitting on the ledge in front of their school. Usually it's the place where kids meet their friends and have some fun talking and joking. But today no one is laughing. Everyone looks shocked and upset, and some of the kids look like they have been crying.

It's the first day of school, and the word is spreading that Jennifer Greenleaf, one of the best athletes in the whole school, was killed in a car crash over the Labor Day weekend. No one can believe it.

Jody and Jennifer had been friends since kindergarten. They lived on the same block and were always on the same school bus. Jody's parents heard the news last evening and told Jody what had happened. Jennifer and her family had been coming back from a weekend trip to a nearby lake, and an 18-wheeler truck slammed into the back of their car. Everyone in the family was hurt, but Jennifer was the only one who died.

Cheryl keeps saying over and over, "I can't believe it; I can't believe it. How could Jennifer be dead? It's impossible."

Ben says, "You better believe it, because it's true. You can't deny it."

Josh keeps repeating, "It's so unfair."

Jody's eyes are brimming with tears. She says, "Jennifer had this dream. Every time she came over to my house, we'd hang out in my room and talk about what we were going to do when we grew up. She always said she was going to go to college on a basketball scholarship, and then play on the U.S. Olympic team. We talked about it a million times."

Carrie doesn't say anything. She just keeps crying silently. Finally Ben says, "We better go inside. I heard that there's going to be a special assembly, and the principal is going to make an announcement to the whole school."

ACCIDENTAL DEATH

Accidents are one of the three most common causes of death for teenagers. For kids up to the age of 14, it is the most common cause of death. Accidental deaths are always shocking because they happen without warning. An accident is always a surprise, and we have no way to control its occurrence, or to prepare for it.

When a young person like Jennifer dies in an accident, it is extremely difficult for everyone. In addition to the feelings of sadness that are typical when a death occurs at any age, there are also feelings of anger. There is anger that a young person's life was cut short before that person had a chance to reach his or her goals. There is anger for a friendship lost.

Accidental death also causes fear and anxiety. The random nature of accidental death makes everyone feel less safe. If it could happen to a friend, could it also

Because an accidental death is so sudden and unexpected, it can be especially painful and difficult to accept.

happen to you? Jennifer was killed in a car crash, so some of her friends might be wary of cars for a while. When someone you know is killed in a plane crash, you might become anxious about flying. Fortunately these fears and anxieties lessen over time. But they are a natural reaction to an accidental death.

FINDING SUPPORT

Carrie, Jody, Cheryl, Josh, and Ben have been doing something that helps. They have been talking with one another about Jennifer's death. They have been sharing their feelings and helping each other to cope. In other words, they have become a support group for each other.

When they go into school, their principal will hold an assembly, so everyone will have a chance to be together. That will be a comfort. The school counselors probably

After a death a support group can help people share
feelings, comfort each other, and heal together.

will be on hand to talk with those kids who are most upset by the news. Other groups of friends like the one in
the story will come together for support and comfort.

People generally pull together in a time of tragedy. A
school can sometimes be like a very large family helping
you to feel more secure and safe in the face of a tragedy,
such as the accidental death of someone your own age.

Nothing can reduce the shock and pain of losing a
young person. But having a group of friends with whom
to share your grief makes it a little easier to bear. Also,
knowing that there are grown-ups at your school who
care deeply and who are there to support you can be
very comforting.

After some time has passed, you and your friends
may want to prepare some kind of memorial ceremony
for your friend. It is a positive way to remember the
friendship you shared.

SUICIDE

Mike's closest friends—Rick, Stu, and Joey—are sprawled out on the floor in Joey's living room. Mike, who was only 12, has committed suicide, and no one can believe it! His friends keep saying the same things over and over: "I don't believe it." "It's not possible." "Why, why, why?" "Why didn't he tell us that he was in such bad shape?" "I just wish I could talk to him right now. I know I could talk him out of it."

Rick says, "Mike was such a great guy. He was real smart, but he didn't brag about it."

Joey adds, "I knew that he had a few problems with family rules and stuff, but doesn't everybody?"

"Yeah," Rick says. "He was crazy about his little sister. He was always saying what a great gymnast she was going to be."

Everyone is quiet for a while. They are trying to figure out what made Mike unhappy enough to take his own life. Then Stu says, "You know, Mike wanted to please everybody. And he would get angry at himself if he thought he had let someone down. Sometimes it was annoying. He'd feel bad about the silliest little thing. I used to tell him to cool it when he was that way. Maybe he finally felt so bad about something that he couldn't handle it."

Joey answers, "Yeah, I noticed that about him, too. Maybe you're right."

Rick says, "I guess we should go over to Mike's house now and see his family."

Joey says, "I suppose we have to. It's going to be terrible. I won't know what to say."

The other boys nod in agreement. They put on their jackets and shuffle out the front door with their heads down. They look as sad as they feel.

The boys are facing a difficult moment—having to find the words to express their feelings to members of a grieving family. The fact is, there are probably no perfect words, no one right way to handle the situation. Their visit to the home of the family, if only to shake hands, give a hug, or say a few words, such as "I'm sorry," will be enough. The family will find great comfort in a simple show of support.

ABOUT SUICIDE

Suicide is the act of taking one's own life. The methods may vary, but the end result is the same—a needless death. Of all the ways in which a loved one dies, suicide is probably the one that is most difficult to understand, to accept, and to talk about.

Suicide is one of the three leading causes of death for teenagers. The other two are accidents and murder. All three are violent and terrible. In the United States, about

Preteen and Teen Suicides, Ages 10–14		
Year	Number of Suicides for Year	Number of Suicides Each Day
1980	800	2.2
1990	1,500	4.1
1992	1,700	4.7

Source: *Statistical Abstract of the United States, 1992* (U.S. Department of Commerce).

Suicide is one of the three leading causes of death for teenagers.

5,000 young people commit suicide each year. Sometimes they attempt suicide but are found in time to prevent death. A suicide attempt is a clear signal that the person is asking for help to overcome the problems that made him or her desperate enough to want to die. Among high school–age people, there are between 100 and 200 attempted suicides for every one that results in death.

HOW SUICIDE AFFECTS THOSE LEFT BEHIND

No matter how bad the problems seemed to the person who took his or her own life, suicide was the worst solution imaginable. Problems usually can be solved. But death puts an end to all the possibilities. With the finality of death, the problems are gone, but so are all the dreams of future happiness and success. After a suicide, the only thing left is the terrible pain that friends and family must deal with.

At the beginning of this chapter, Rick, Stu, and Joey were trying to sort out their feelings and thoughts about

Mike's suicide. They were going through a process that everyone who is left behind goes through after a suicide.

What were they feeling? They were feeling a terrible sadness and sense of loss. They were feeling grief. Their friend had died before he had a chance to live his life fully. He would never again be there to share the fun they had together as boys and would have had as young men. They were feeling angry that he hadn't confided in them about how troubled he was. They were shocked. Although they were Mike's closest friends, they had no idea that he was in such despair. They probably felt guilty for not noticing.

They all shared feelings of disbelief. It didn't seem real that someone they had known for such a long time was no longer alive. It was hard to comprehend the finality of it. They were feeling sympathy for Mike's family and anxiety about having to take part in the family's grief.

Rick, Stu, and Joey were trying to understand why Mike had killed himself. It is always so difficult for those left behind to understand why someone would take his or her own life. Often you can ponder the "why" question for years, but no answer seems good enough. For most people, suicide is not understandable.

The boys were starting to ask questions that will come up over and over as they try to cope with Mike's suicide. Could they have done anything to prevent it? Why hadn't they noticed that their friend was feeling so bad? Had his family seen any signs? Should they have been better at recognizing symptoms? Did Mike give any clues that they missed?

What Leads to Suicide?

The factors that lead to suicide are different for each person. Some possible factors are listed here:

▶ **Family Problems.** Some kids are expected to follow too many rules at home, or not enough; some see alcoholism, violence, or sexual abuse in the family; parents may divorce, causing their children to feel confused or unloved.

▶ **Communication Problems.** Some kids feel that they have no one with whom to share their innermost thoughts, no one to confide in, no one they can trust.

▶ **Self-esteem Problems.** Some kids don't feel good about themselves; they may not feel that they are good-looking enough, athletic enough, or smart enough; they think that they disappoint their parents, their peers, or even themselves.

▶ **Problems with Drugs or Alcohol.** Some kids begin abusing drugs; they may become addicted; and they may commit crimes to get money for their habits.

▶ **Problems with Fear or Anxiety.** Some kids have trouble controlling their fears about school, about growing up and having adult responsibilities, or about a particular problem in their lives.

▶ **Problems with Depression.** Some kids have periods of depression when they feel low, unhappy, even desperate.

▶ **Problems with Anger.** Kids may feel angry at themselves or at others.

The common thread that runs through all of the items on this list is the feeling of being overwhelmed by problems for which there seem to be no solutions. But solutions can be found. There are places to go when you need help. Some of these are listed at the back of this book.

People who are thinking about suicide do, in fact, often provide clues that can be recognized as danger signals. If you are worried that a friend may be thinking about suicide, you should immediately tell an adult who can provide help. There are warning signs that someone is thinking about suicide. The person may:

▶ Talk about death or about hurting himself or herself—and perhaps even mention a specific plan.

▶ Have pills, a weapon, or another means of committing suicide.

▶ Give away some of his or her belongings.

▶ Appear happy for no apparent reason after being depressed for a long time.

Don't be afraid to ask for help. It is better to be wrong about your friend's intentions than to find that it is too late to help.

FEELING GRIEF

Melissa is 12 years old. She lives with her mother and father and her 15-year-old brother, Max, in a small, midwestern city. Melissa is in middle school, and Max is in high school.

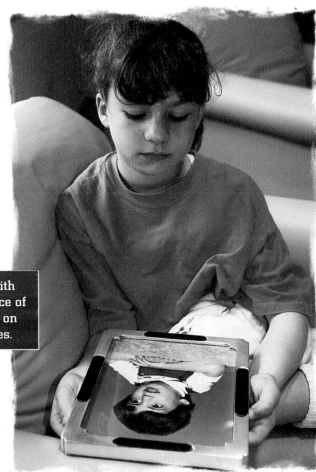

One way of dealing with the permanent absence of a loved one is to hold on to the happy memories.

There used to be three children in the family, but last year there was a terrible accident. Tony, who was seven years old, was playing catch with a friend in the front yard. He was allowed to do that as long as he stayed inside the fence. But his ball went over the fence into the street. Tony, forgetting the rule, ran after the ball. He was struck by a delivery truck and killed instantly.

Tony was the baby of the family. Everyone adored him and enjoyed his funny ways. He was happy to have a big sister and brother, and he always wanted to do whatever they did. He liked to be independent, and he was so pleased when he was given permission to play outside without another family member watching him.

After Tony's death the family went through a period of intense grief. His mom and dad took a month off from work. Melissa and Max went back to school after a week, but they didn't stay for after-school sports or clubs. They came right home to be with their parents. Sometimes friends came over to visit, but it was a pretty sad time.

Now it's a year later. Everyone is still grieving, but in a different way. Often, after dinner, the family sits around the kitchen table and tells stories about Tony's funny antics. They laugh when they remember the things he used to do and say.

At other times each person grieves alone. Tony's dad thinks of him every time Melissa smiles, because their smiles were so much alike. Tony's mom recently gave away his toys and clothes to the homeless shelter

Doing something good in the name of a lost loved one
helps ease the pain and keep the person's memory alive.

downtown. It made her feel a little better to know that other children would be able to use them. Melissa remembers how sweet and fresh Tony looked in his pajamas after his bath. Max often thinks about how happy Tony was when he read him a favorite story.

There are still pictures of Tony all over the house, alone and with his brother and sister. No one wants to forget that he was once part of their family.

THE PROCESS OF GRIEVING

When you first lose someone you love, the emotional pain you feel is very strong. The closer you have been to the person who has died, the more intense your feelings of loss and grief will be. When you wake up in the morning, a feeling of sadness comes over you as soon as you open your eyes. When you go to bed at night, those intense feelings are likely to return. Sometimes you may even feel physically ill. Your stomach may be queasy, or your head may hurt. Emotional distress can and often does cause physical symptoms.

Like Tony's family, people often can't go about their daily routines right after a death. They need to allow themselves time for grieving. It is really important to do that.

After you experience the death of someone close to you, it is natural to think that life will never return to normal and that sad feelings will permanently replace happier ones. Over time, however, those intense feelings of sadness become less strong, no matter how much you love the person who died. The old saying "Time is a great healer" is true. While the amount of time it takes to heal emotionally is different for each individual, eventually most people learn to accept their losses and move on with their lives.

EXPRESSING GRIEF

People express grief in many different ways. Some do it very openly, weeping and talking about their sorrow. Some people become very quiet and cry only in private. Still others keep their grief deep inside. It may seem as if they are not touched at all by the death. People who are not able to express their grief in some way often have delayed and more severe reactions later in life.

Sharing your sorrow with someone who is also grieving can help both of you cope with the loss.

Communicating with people who share your sorrow is very important. It is the first step in the healing process. Tony's family was able to do that. Talking about Tony made them feel closer to one another, and their remembrances kept Tony's memory alive.

Some people have difficulty expressing their grief. If you are one of those people, try sharing your feelings with just one other person. It really helps in the long run if you let your sorrow out sooner rather than later.

DENYING DEATH

In this book we have talked about the difficulty of communicating about death. Why is it so hard? One reason is that you often go into a kind of shock when you are faced with the death of someone close. The reality is so painful to accept that your emotions shut down for a while. In other words, you deny the reality. This kind of denial is natural and usually goes away fairly quickly, so that you can begin to grieve and then to heal.

There is another kind of denial that is important to know about. In the United States, we have become pretty far removed from seeing death as a natural part of the life cycle. We know that doctors use life-support machines to keep people alive for years. We are taught to believe that a cure for every disease is just around the corner.

Although our parents tell us that death is natural, they also try to shield us from the sadness that death brings. Adults often won't even say the word *death* in the presence of children. They hide death behind phrases like "Uncle Ned has passed away" or "Grandma isn't with us anymore." In our society children do not regularly attend funerals, as they do in other places around the world.

We also form a strange view of death from television, movies, and comic strips. On the one hand, we may hear so much in the news about death caused by war and other violence that we become numb to it. On the other hand, we see cartoon characters encounter many things that in real life would kill them—explosions, gunshots, beatings—but they bounce right up again, as good as new.

This kind of cultural denial of death is simply unrealistic. Keeping death at arm's length, treating death as something to avoid talking about, leaves us unprepared for this final event in everyone's life. While some denial may help us deal with the shock of death at first, in the long run it prevents us from accepting death and healing our grief.

COPING WITH DEATH

Even though it was a Monday afternoon and not a holiday, Joanna's house was crowded with relatives and friends. Joanna, who is 11, had just returned from the funeral service and burial of her uncle Jeff. Uncle Jeff was her mother's younger brother. Joanna's mother and Jeff were close in age and had grown up feeling almost like twins. Joanna's mother had taken care of Uncle Jeff during his year-long illness with leukemia. She was at his bedside when he died.

Now Joanna, her father and mother, her older sister Olivia, and her grandparents were sitting shivah in her house from Monday, when Uncle Jeff was buried, until Friday evening, when the Jewish Sabbath would begin. Shivah is a mourning tradition in the Jewish religion.

Each day the family would sit together and share their memories of Jeff. Sometimes, in spite of their sadness, they would laugh, remembering jokes that Jeff used to tell. He had been such a funny man.

Every evening during the shivah, friends would arrive. People would bring food, so that the family would not have to bother with cooking during their time of mourning.

One night, Joanna's mother came into her bedroom and sat on her bed. Joanna knew that her mother was feeling very sad, so she put her arms around her and gave her a long, tight hug. As they were talking, Joanna asked, "What do people who aren't Jewish do after someone dies?"

Her mother explained that every culture has mourning traditions that are followed after a family member dies. She said, "Do you remember when Jessie's mother died?" Jessie was her mother's best friend at work. Joanna nodded. Her mother said, "I went to a viewing for Jessie's mother."

"What's that?" Joanna asked, very puzzled.

Her mother answered, "Nowadays, in some Christian religions, friends and relatives may come to sit with the mourners and comfort them before the funeral. Sometimes people look at the dead person in his or her coffin. It's a way for people to come together to comfort the family of the dead person."

Four months ago Reggie's best friend, Robert, died as the result of a bicycle accident. Ever since the accident, Reggie felt bad every morning. His stomach felt like it was tied in knots, and he felt depressed as he thought about the school day ahead. School wasn't any fun without Robert, and weekends were the pits.

It had rained hard the day before the accident, and Robert's bike had skidded on wet leaves. He wasn't wearing his helmet. Reggie had always tried to make him put it on when they went biking together, but

Robert said it made his head sweat. When Robert's bike skidded, he fell and hit his head on a rock. He was in a coma for a month, and then he died.

This morning Reggie woke up at his usual time, 6:30 A.M., but today was different. He jumped out of bed and put on his favorite clothes. Today Reggie is going to hang a plaque in Robert's memory in the school. Reggie had thought up the idea, and he had collected money from Robert's friends and teachers.

The students had planned an assembly program. They had written speeches, songs, and poems honoring Robert, who had been very well liked. Some of the songs and poems were pretty funny; some were serious and sad. Robert's parents and his two older brothers were planning to attend the assembly.

Reggie felt good about being the first speaker at the ceremony. For the first time since the accident, Reggie looked forward to the day.

CUSTOMS AND RITUALS OF HONOR AND REMEMBRANCE

Joanna and her family were taking part in shivah, a custom in the Jewish religion. They also talked about a viewing and a wake, which are Christian customs. Everywhere in the world, people have customs and rituals that are performed when a person dies. These traditions vary from one culture to another, but they all have a common purpose. They honor the dead person and comfort his or her family and friends.

Honoring a loved one in a special ceremony is a good way to express your feelings for that person.

Some customs and rituals come from the religious tradition of the dead person. But some memorial ceremonies are not religious. They are rituals that are created by friends and family to honor a person for his or her work or special talent. Reggie's school assembly for his friend Robert is an example of a nonreligious memorial.

Sometimes when a famous musician dies, friends come together to play music in his or her honor. Sometimes when an actor dies, other actors come together to remember the roles he or she played.

Another way to honor or remember someone who has died is to make a charitable contribution to an organization that the person supported when he or she was alive. The ways to honor and remember a person who has died are as varied as the people themselves.

FUNERALS

A funeral is another ritual or custom that accompanies a death. It is a ceremony that goes with burial in the ground or cremation (burning into ashes) of the physical body of

The customs and rituals that follow a death help us put closure on a person's life.

a person who has died. Burial may be preceded by a religious service or followed later by a memorial gathering.

Like other rituals, burial and cremation customs vary according to religion and culture. But regardless of the form of the ceremony, the purpose is the same. A funeral is the closing of a person's life. Seeing the body of a loved one buried in the ground, or witnessing a cremation, can be a very painful experience. But it helps people understand the finality of death.

COPING WITH LOSS

No one is ever fully prepared for the death of a loved one. If an older person dies, you may be more accepting of the death, but the sense of loss you feel still hurts. If a parent or a young person dies, the shock and sense of loss are greater. In other words, the death of a loved one at any age is one of the most painful experiences we endure as human beings.

As soon as you are faced with the death of a loved one, you begin to cope with your loss. Coping is a process that includes several stages. And it takes time.

Some experts who have studied grief and mourning say that people who have lost someone close to them go through three stages: chaos, expression, and understanding. Let's briefly examine each stage so that you know what to expect:

▶ **Chaos.** The time immediately following the death of a loved one is a period of confusion. You may feel numb, shocked, frightened, physically ill, or unable to believe that the death is real. You may want to be alone and withdraw from your friends and family.

▶ **Expression.** Soon you should be able to share your thoughts and feelings about the death. It is very important to allow yourself to do this. Crying, talking about the dead person, and expressing the emotions you are feeling through words or actions will help you to release your pain. If it seems too difficult for you to do this, seek help from a trusted adult.

▶ **Understanding.** When enough time has passed, and you have given full expression to your grief, you will realize that you can move on with your life and give your love to those around you who have not died.

Passing into the stage of understanding doesn't mean that you forget the person you have lost. David Crenshaw, who wrote a book called *Bereavement: Counseling the Grieving Throughout the Life Cycle*, says that no one ever completely recovers from the loss of someone he or she deeply loved. Recovery from grief means that you can face and bear the loss. The author writes that you are permanently changed as a result of the experience, and that some of the changes may be positive. For example, you may discover great strength within yourself.

STRATEGIES FOR COPING

Reggie finally found a strategy for coping with the loss of his friend Robert. By organizing the memorial assembly and arranging for the plaque, he was able to find a positive expression for his grief. He also created a way for other friends to express their feelings.

One good way to reach the stage of understanding and acceptance of death is through creative expression. For some people, it may be writing about their thoughts and feelings in a journal or diary, which can always remain private. For others, writing a story or newspaper article may relieve their grief. Others may write songs or perform music. Someone else may draw, paint, or create a dance.

Another strategy is to find release by helping someone in need. Working in a soup kitchen or volunteering at a day-care center or nursing home takes you away from your personal pain for a time and helps you focus on others.

Playing sports or participating in other physical activities is another helpful strategy. Exercising your body relieves tension and helps you stay healthy. Exercise also uses energy, so it can help you sleep better if you are having trouble sleeping.

There are many ways in which people can refocus their energies and reduce the pain of their losses.

Using drugs or alcohol to numb the emotional pain you are feeling is, at best, a very short-term remedy that briefly masks feelings. Alcohol and drugs don't help you go through the stages of grief or deal with your feelings in a healthy way. And they may bring the additional problem of coping with an addiction.

Chances are, if you are reading this book, it is because someone who was close to you has died. We have tried to give a realistic picture of what it feels like to experience death—what to expect, what the stages of grief and mourning are like for most people, and the knowledge that eventually you will pass through the sorrow and move on with your life. Knowing that this topic may be hard to read about, we have nevertheless tried not to minimize the sadness and sense of loss that the death of a loved one brings. To do that would have been unfair to you after the experience you have had.

addiction: Uncontrollable dependency on a substance, such as alcohol or another drug.

anxiety: Uneasy concern or worry about something.

coma: A state of deep unconsciousness, usually caused by disease or injury.

cremation: The burning of a dead body to ashes.

depression: Strong feeling of sadness or gloom.

funeral: A ceremony that is performed when a person dies; usually accompanied by burial or cremation.

living will: A legal document that states a person's wish not to be kept alive by machines in the event of an injury or illness from which she or he will not recover.

self-esteem: A feeling of one's self-worth.

substance abuse: Harmfully excessive intake of a substance, such as alcohol or other drugs.

terminal illness: Illness that ends in death.

therapist: Someone who treats diseases and disabilities or helps people cope with emotional problems.

will: A legal document that states how a person wishes his or her belongings to be distributed after death.

WHERE TO GO FOR HELP

Organizations

Canadian Mental Health Association
1-613-737-7791

Children's Hospice International
700 Princess Street
Lower Level
Alexandria, VA 22314

Compassionate Friends
P.O. Box 3696
Oak Brook, IL 60522
1-312-990-0010

This is a self-help organization for parents and siblings of a child who has died. It has local groups in many areas of the country. Look in the telephone directory white pages for a group near you.

Students Against Driving Drunk (SADD)
P.O. Box 800
Marlboro, MA 01752

Modeled after Mothers Against Drunk Driving (MADD), this group works to keep young people who have been drinking off the road, so that they don't kill themselves or others through drunk driving accidents.

Suicide Information and Education Centre
1615 Tenth Avenue, SW
Calgary, ABT3C 0J7
Canada
1-403-245-3900

THEOS
1301 Clark Building
717 Liberty Avenue
Pittsburgh, PA 15222
1-412-471-7779

THEOS stands for "They Help Each Other Spiritually." This group was formed by men and women and their families who were working to rebuild their lives after the untimely death of a spouse or parent. There are local THEOS chapters nationwide. Look for them in the white pages of your telephone book.

Fiction

Campbell, James A. *The Secret Places.* Centering Corporation, 1992.

Deaver, Julie Reece. *Say Goodnight, Gracie.* HarperCollins, 1988.

Hesse, Karen. *Phoenix Rising.* Henry Holt and Company, 1994.

Hurwin, Davida Wills. *A Time for Dancing.* Little, Brown, 1995.

Jordan, Mary Kay. *Losing Uncle Tim.* Albert Whitman, 1989.

Paterson, Katherine. *Bridge to Terabithia.* HarperCollins, 1977.

Tiffault, Benette W. *A Quilt for Elizabeth.* Centering Corporation, 1992.

Nonfiction

Crenshaw, David A. *Bereavement: Counseling the Grieving Throughout the Life Cycle.* Crossroad, 1995.

Fayerweather Street School Staff. *The Kids' Book About Death and Dying.* Edited by Eric E. Rofes. Little, Brown, 1985.

Gardner, Sandra. *Teenage Suicide.* Julian Messner, 1990.

Gootman, Marilyn E. *When a Friend Dies: A Book for Teens About Grieving and Healing.* Free Spirit, 1994.

Grollman, Earl A. *Straight Talk About Death for Teenagers: How to Cope with Losing Someone You Love.* Beacon Press, 1993.

Heegaard, Marge Eaton. *Coping with Death and Grief.* Lerner, 1990.

Krementz, Jill. *How It Feels When a Parent Dies.* Alfred A. Knopf, 1981.

LeShan, Eda. *Learning to Say Good-bye: When a Parent Dies.* Macmillan, 1976.

Richter, Elizabeth. *Losing Someone You Love: When a Brother or Sister Dies.* G. P. Putnam's Sons, 1986.

INDEX

abandonment, feelings of, 17, 19
acceptance, 8, 20, 34, 36, 41
accidents, 16, 22, 23, 32, 38
addiction, 29, 44
alcohol, 29, 44
anger, 4, 8, 14, 17, 22, 25, 28, 29
anxiety, 18, 22, 23, 28, 29

burial, 37, 40

cancer, 10, 14
coma, 15
comfort, 8, 19, 20, 23–24, 26, 38,
    39–40
communication, 11, 14, 16, 19, 20,
    23–24, 34–35, 42
confusion, 4, 42
coping with death, 5, 19–20, 23–24,
    35, 37–39, 42–44
counselors, 19, 23–24
cremation, 40–41

death as part of life cycle, 8, 9, 36
denial, 18, 35–36. *See also* disbelief
depression, 29, 38
disbelief, 4, 18, 21, 25, 28, 42
divorce, 29
drugs, 29, 44

embarrassment, 18–19
emotions, 4, 8, 14, 17–19, 20, 22–23,
    27–28, 42
expressing oneself, 19, 21–22, 26,
    29, 34–35, 42, 43

family unity, 14–15, 19–20
fear, 4, 14, 22–23, 29, 42
funerals, 6, 7, 36, 37–38, 40–41

grieving, 4, 12, 16, 17–19, 23–24, 32–35
guilt, 28

help, asking for, 19, 30, 42
helplessness, 18
honoring the dead, 39–40, 43

legal issues, 10–11, 12
loneliness, 12

loss, sense of, 4, 9, 14, 22, 24, 28, 41,
    44

medication, 7, 10

pain, emotional, 8, 17, 23, 24, 27,
    33–34
parents, death of, 13, 15–20
physical exercise, 43
preparations, making, 11–12, 15–16,
    22

recovery process, 20, 27–28, 32–33,
    35, 39–40, 42–43
relief, death as, 9, 16–17
religious customs, 19, 37–38, 39
remembering, positive, 24, 32–33,
    35, 37, 39–40
responsibility, 14, 15, 29
rituals, 37–38, 39–41

self-esteem, 29
separation, process of, 11–12, 16
sharing feelings, 11, 20, 21–22, 23,
    24, 35
shock, 9, 16, 18, 21, 22, 24, 28, 35,
    41, 42
sickness, 9–10, 13–17
sleeplessness, 43
stress, 13
sudden death, 9, 16, 21, 22–23
suffering, physical, 10, 14, 17
suicide, 25–30
support, 19–20, 23–24, 26
sympathy, 19, 26, 28

terminal illness, 10, 14–15, 16–17
time (as a healer), 20, 23, 34
treatment, medical, 10–11, 36

understanding, 28, 42

viewing, 6, 38, 39
violence, 26

wills, 12
withdrawal, 34, 42